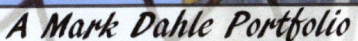
A Mark Dahle Portfolio

The Grasshopper And The Flea

Some Things Never Change

(Fables About Aesop #1)

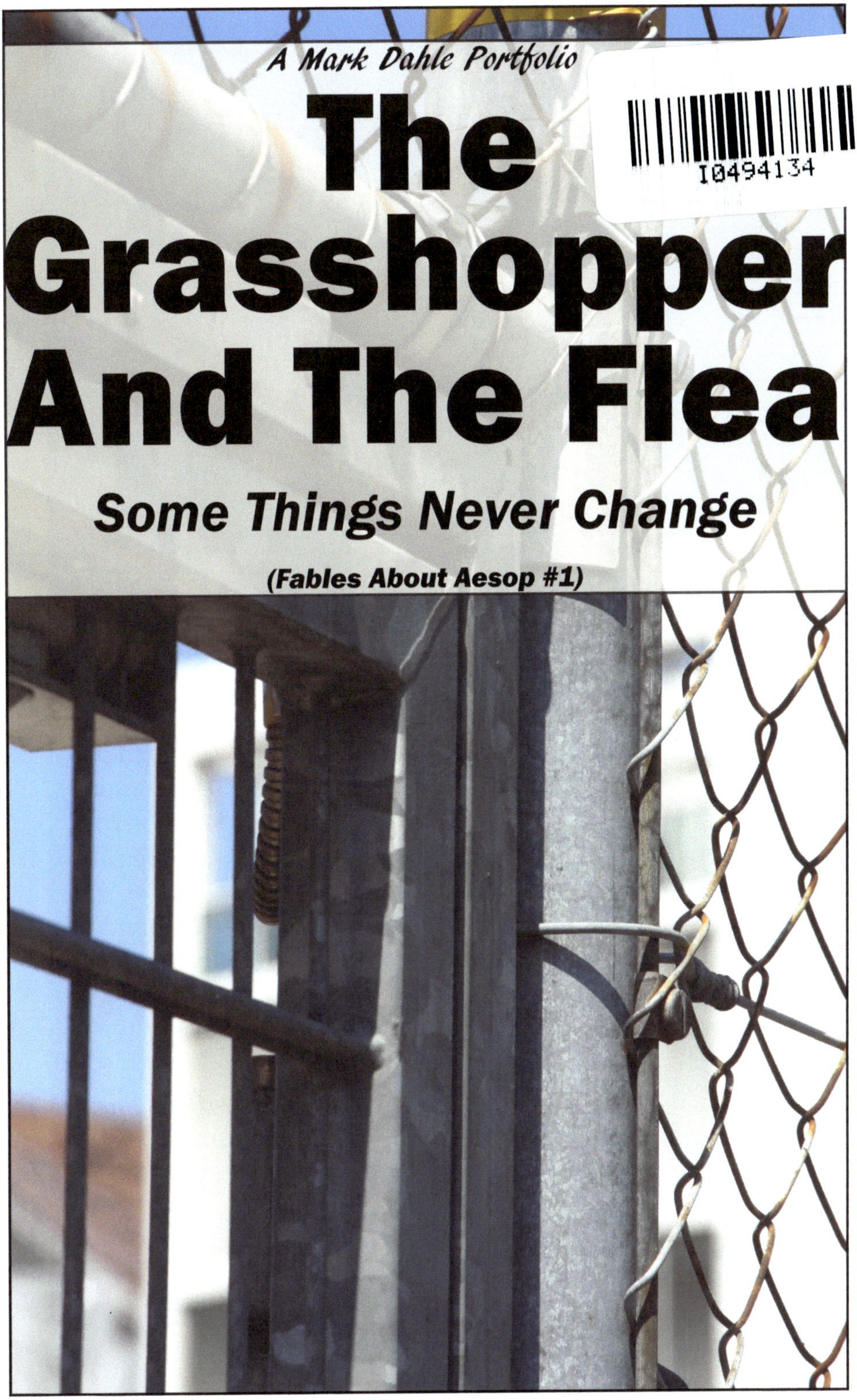

Mark Dahle Portfolios can be read in a few minutes and enjoyed for a lifetime.

Unlike many picture books, the text is not related to the beautiful painting at the right and the photographs that follow. This might seem a little weird at first. One thing that helps is to order more portfolios until you get used to it. In the meantime, feel free to draw your own pictures of grasshoppers and fleas if you like.

This portfolio includes a photo of a brilliant 36 x 24 inch painting (at the right), twenty-six beautiful pictures of fences in Basel, Switzerland, and a story about Aesop having remarkable difficulties writing a fable.

Photographs in this book are available in very limited editions. See http://www.MarkDahle.com for more information and for previews of upcoming portfolios.

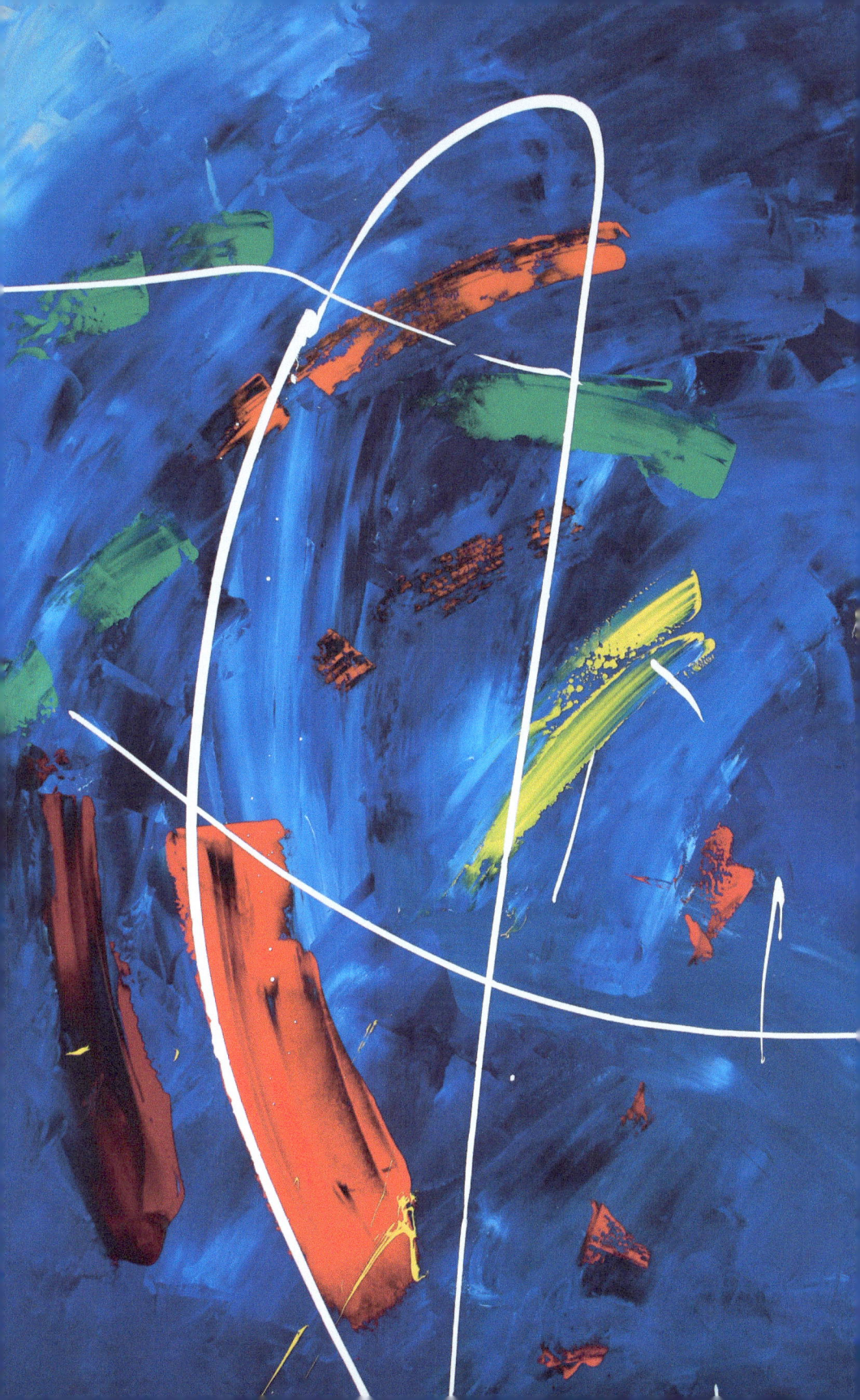

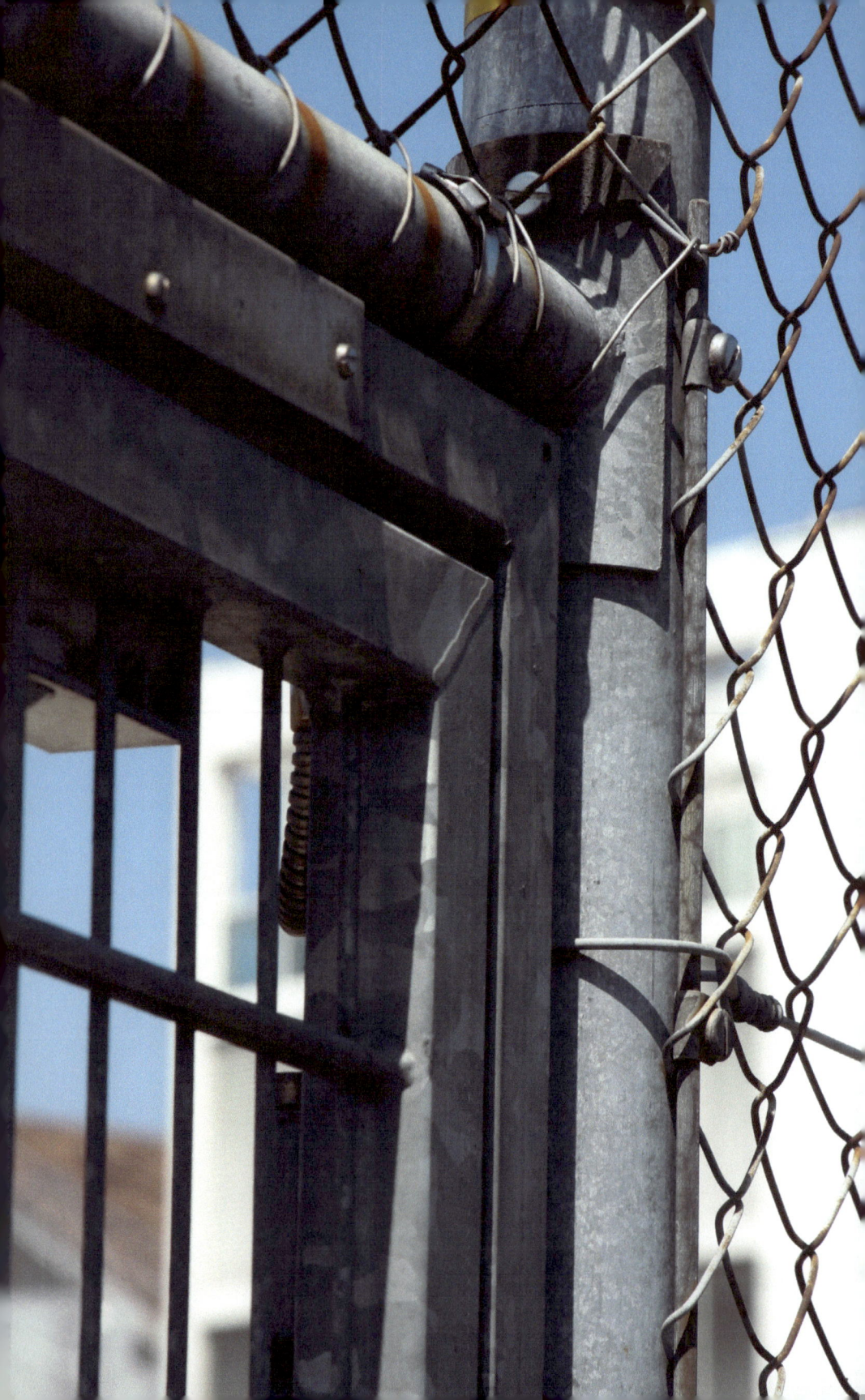

Aesop was worried. He liked the morals at the end of his stories to stay put. But he had just written about a grasshopper and a flea, and the moral was hopping around as much as the two creatures in the story.

Each time he told the story, the moral was slightly different. And Aesop didn't like things to change. Not one bit.

The day had begun like any other. Aesop had been with his children in the morning, then had gone on a walk to deliver mail for his neighbors and to write and think. On the walk he had seen a grasshopper, and that had given him the inspiration for the story.

He had written it as he walked:

> Once there was a grasshopper and a young flea who lived next door to each other. Every morning the flea saw the grasshopper hop away from his house, covering enormous distances. And every morning the flea also hopped away from *his* house. But try as he might, the flea was not able to hop quite as far as the grasshopper.
>
> "When I grow up," the flea said, "I'm going to be a grasshopper."

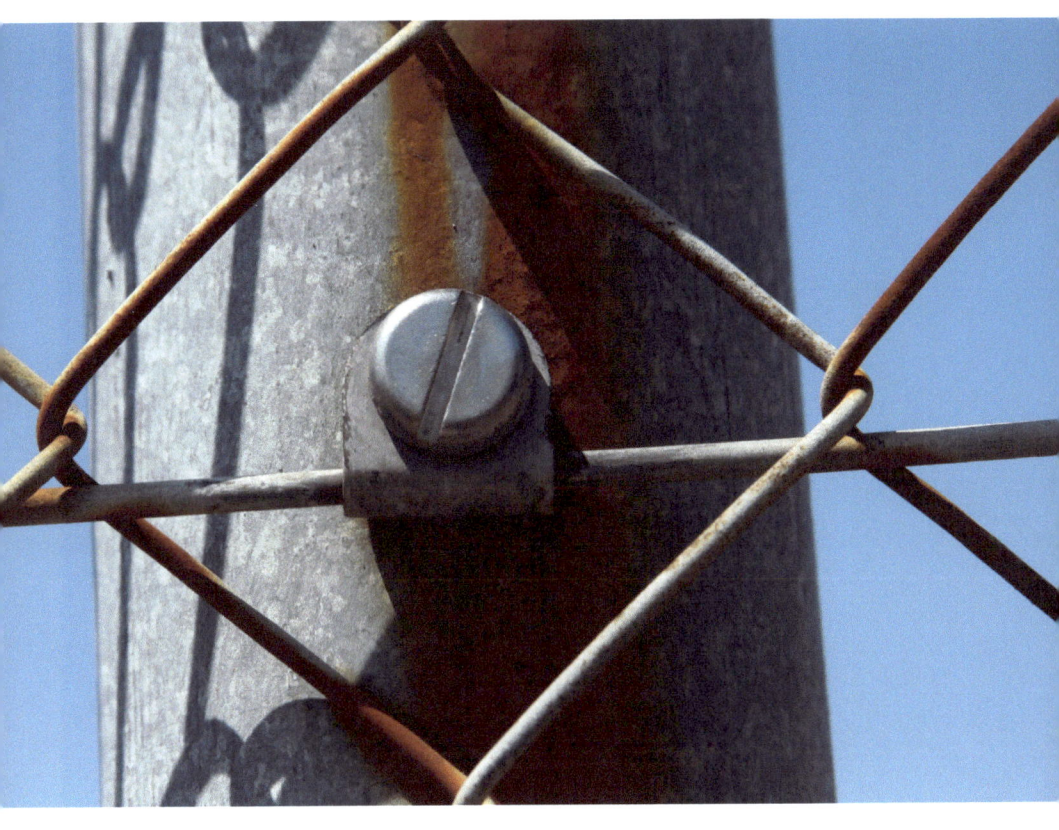

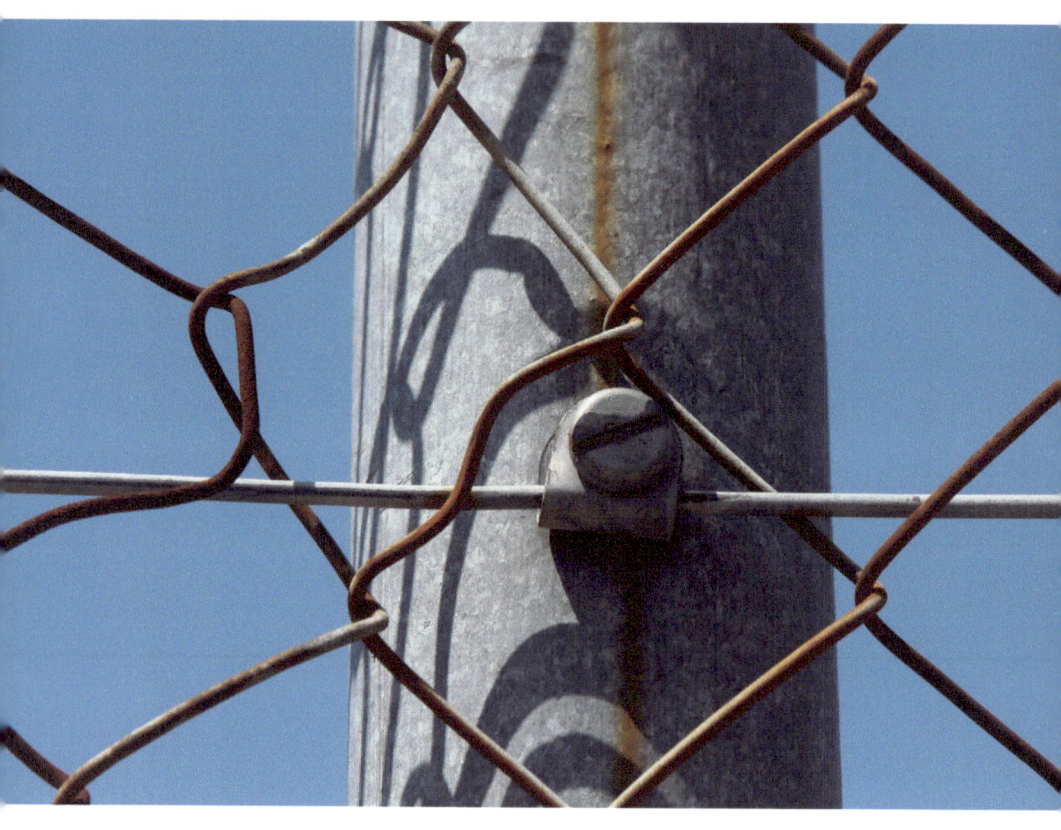

The flea poured all his resources into the quest. He studied the grasshopper every time he saw him. He peppered the grasshopper with questions about technique, diet, and training practices. He copied the grasshopper in every respect he could think of. He read all the grasshopper books he could find. He even joined a club for grasshoppers.

For months the flea worked to be like his neighbor in every detail. But nothing came of his enormous effort. When the flea grew up, he became an adult flea, not an adult grasshopper, and as a result of all his training he hopped rather less well than an ordinary flea. But he kept telling himself he was close to a breakthrough, and just one more day might make all the difference.

The moral of the story is this: You can't become something you're not.

Aesop was quite pleased with his new fable, and couldn't wait to tell it to his children, who were usually delighted to hear his new (and old) stories.

The next morning, when Aesop greeted his children, he told them the new fable.

"And the moral of the story," Aesop said when he was done, "is that some things never change."

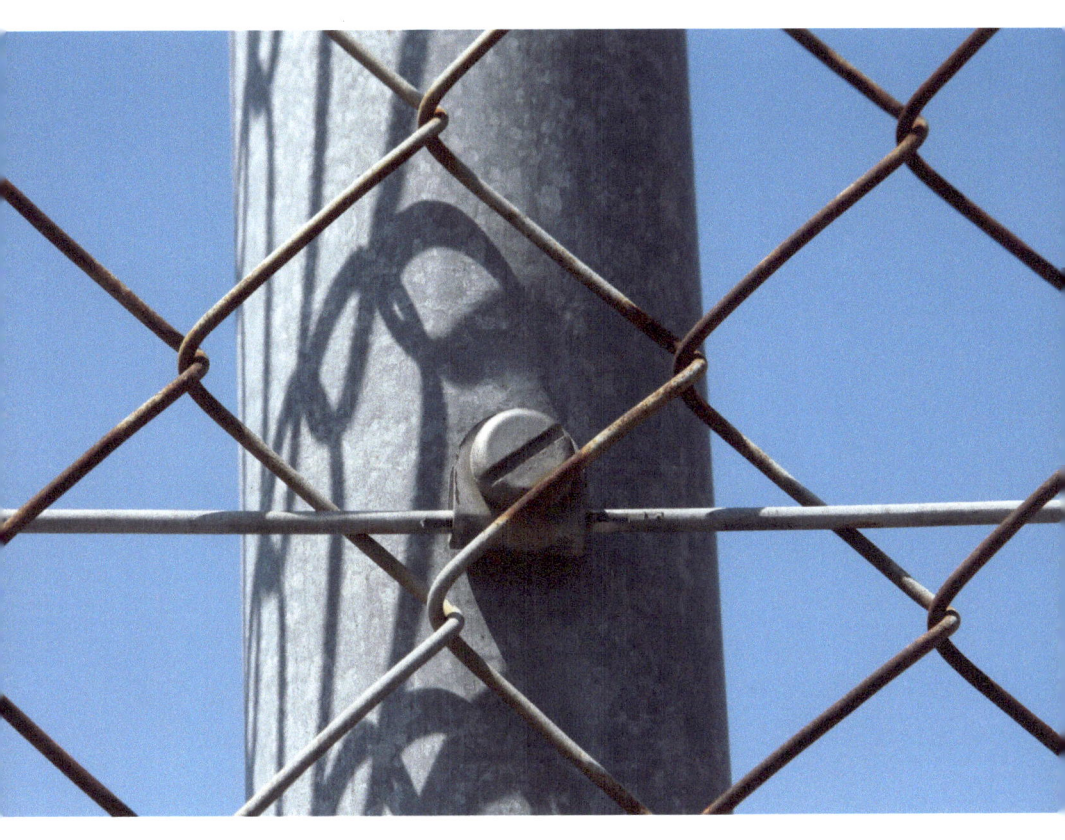

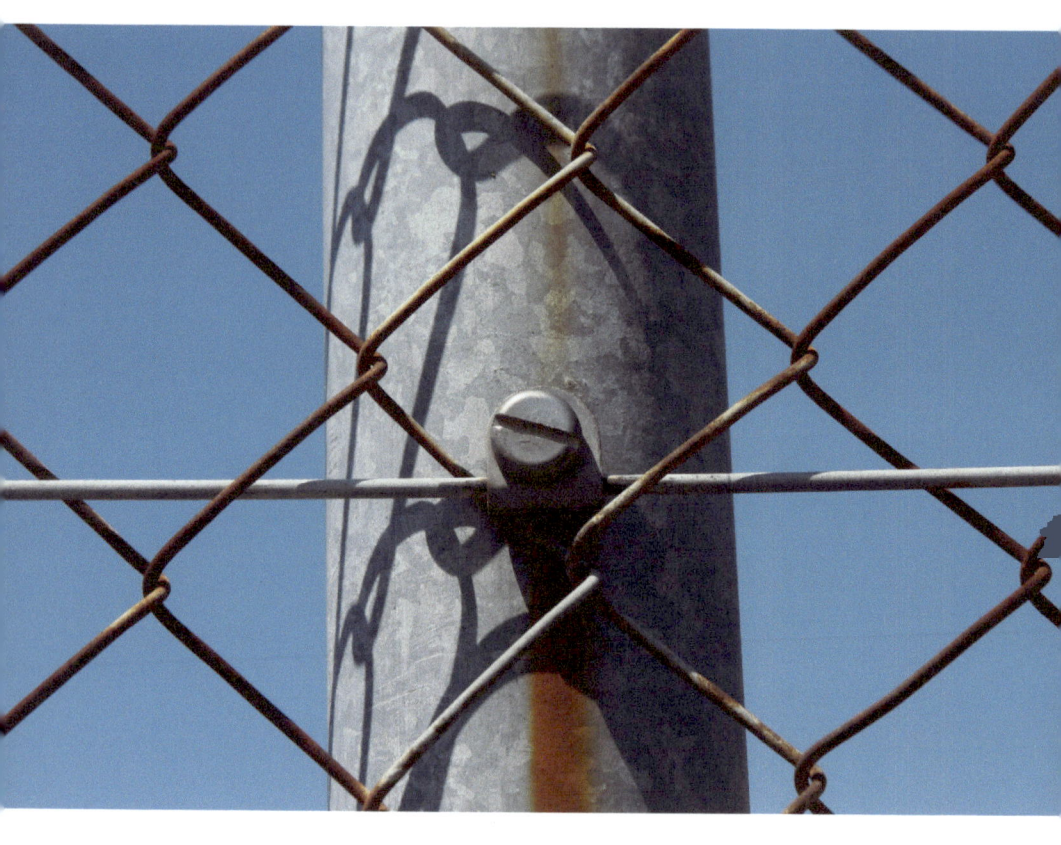

Aesop's children clapped and went out to play. But Aesop did not move from the spot. He had not intended to give the story a different moral. And admittedly, it was not *completely* different. But it was different enough to bother him. Aesop liked things to stay the same. And, overnight, the moral of this story had hopped to a (slightly) new location.

The next morning, Aesop met his children at breakfast and they all begged for a story. "Tell us about the hopping flea!" said Athena, his youngest, who always liked to hear stories more than once. Usually Athena liked to hear the same stories dozens of times.

Aesop told the story again. "And the moral of the story," he said, "is this: If you can't keep up with the Joneses, it may not be your fault."

There was complete silence, except for the sound of Aesop covering his open mouth with his hand. His eyes were wide. He could not believe he'd just said that.

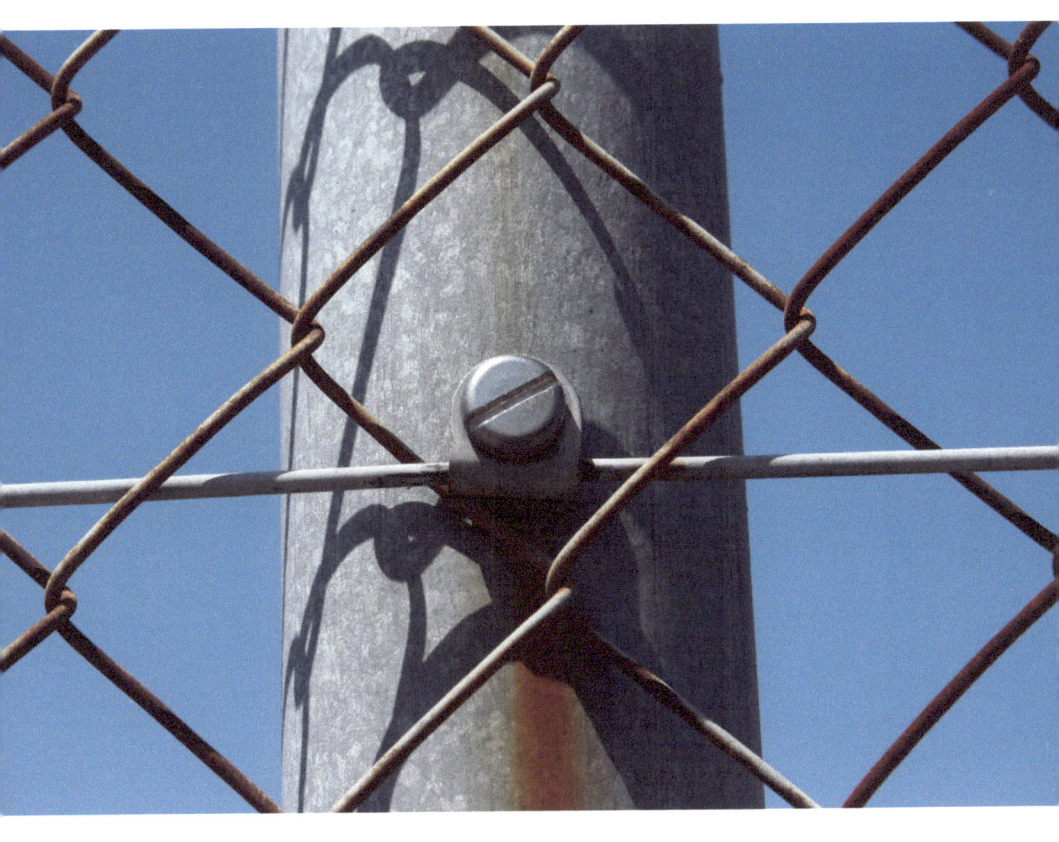

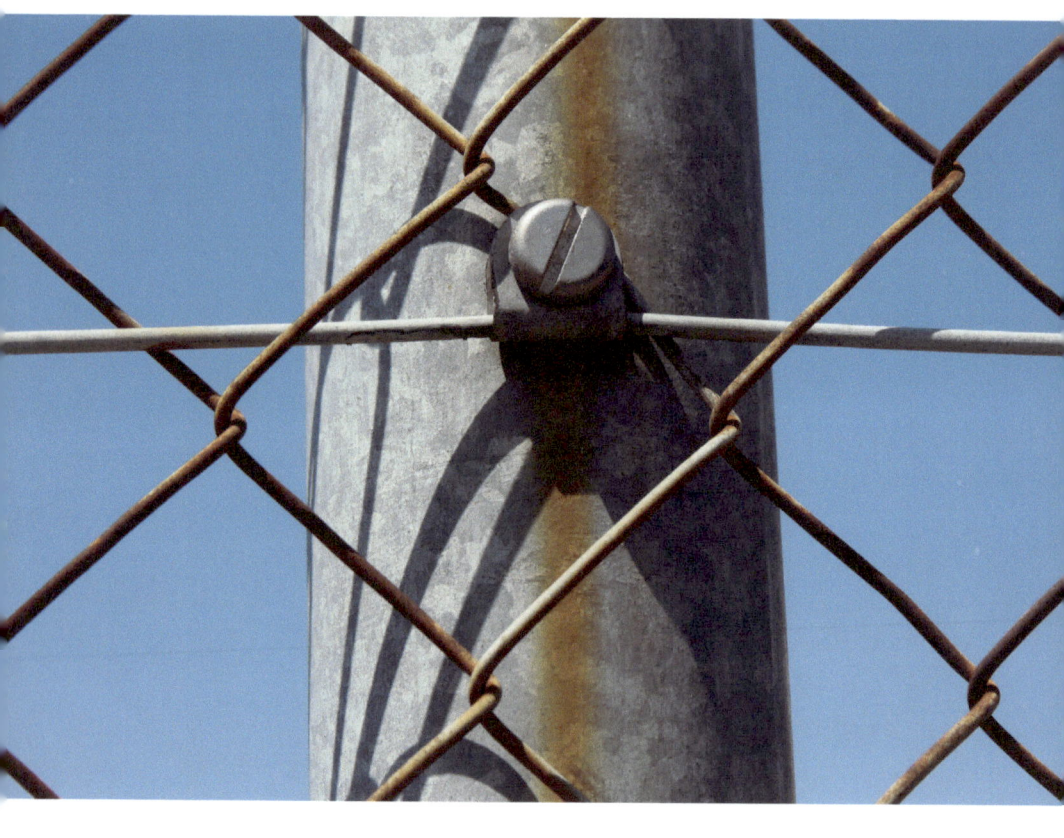

The children couldn't believe it either.
None of them clapped.

"Who are the Joneses?" asked Athena. "That makes no sense at all."

"You're not telling it right," said Alex, his youngest son. "You're supposed to say, 'Some things never change.'"

Aesop was too astonished to reply. He *never* changed the moral of his fables. But this moral had hopped again. Admittedly, it had hopped just a little, but enough so all his children noticed. What if the moral *kept* hopping every time he told the story? In ten or twenty hops, the moral might be someplace radically different from where it had started. What if *all* the morals to his fables started hopping around, just a little? People wouldn't be able to count on his stories for predictable advice. His career as a storyteller might be over. He shuddered.

The next morning the children demanded Aesop tell them the story of the grasshopper and the flea. "But you have to tell it right," said Athena. "No jokes like yesterday," said Alex.

Aesop refused. Never before had he refused his children when they requested a story, but this time he did. He wasn't sure *where* the moral had hopped to over the previous night. All he knew was that it probably wasn't going to be where he or his children expected it. So he told them the fable about the fox and the grapes instead.

The story didn't satisfy them or him, and they left to play, grumbling a little.

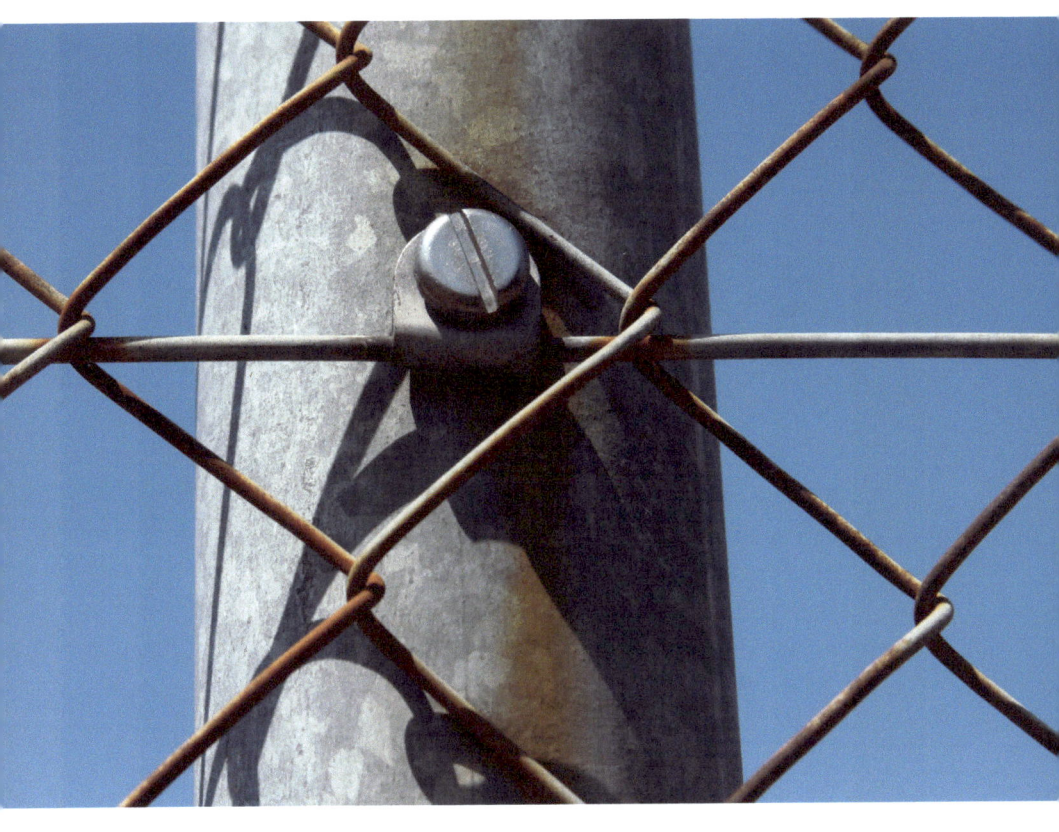

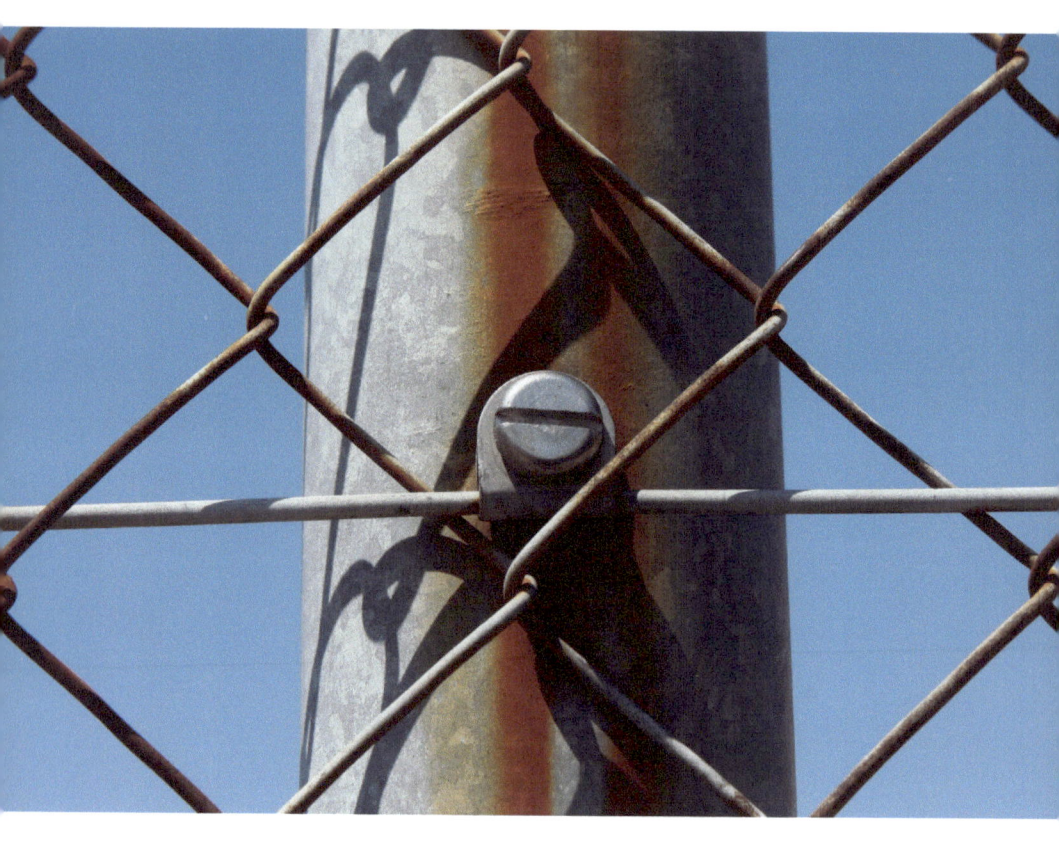

That afternoon Aesop took a walk. His neighbors were used to seeing him practicing his stories on long walks as he delivered mail, but they noticed that today he was more animated than usual.

Aesop was practicing the story of the grasshopper and the flea. He knew Athena would ask for it again, and he wanted to be ready to say it right. So on this walk he was repeating it, over and over, trying to force the moral to be predictable. But each time he came to the moral, something different hopped out of his mouth.

On the first telling of his walk, he had said, "And the moral is this: Do your best and ignore your neighbors."

That caused Aesop to frown, because he loved his neighbors and didn't want to teach his children to disrespect them.

So he started over. When he got to the end he cleared his throat. "The moral is this," he said nervously, hoping to get back to the original. "Some vows are impossible to keep."

He paused, blinking. For a second he couldn't even remember what the moral was *supposed* to be, so he couldn't remember if he'd gotten it right this time or not. He started to smile, thinking at first that he had succeeded. Then he frowned and screamed, "No! No! No! It's supposed to be 'Some things never change!'"

By this time he had completely forgotten the original moral, but at least he remembered what his kids were expecting.

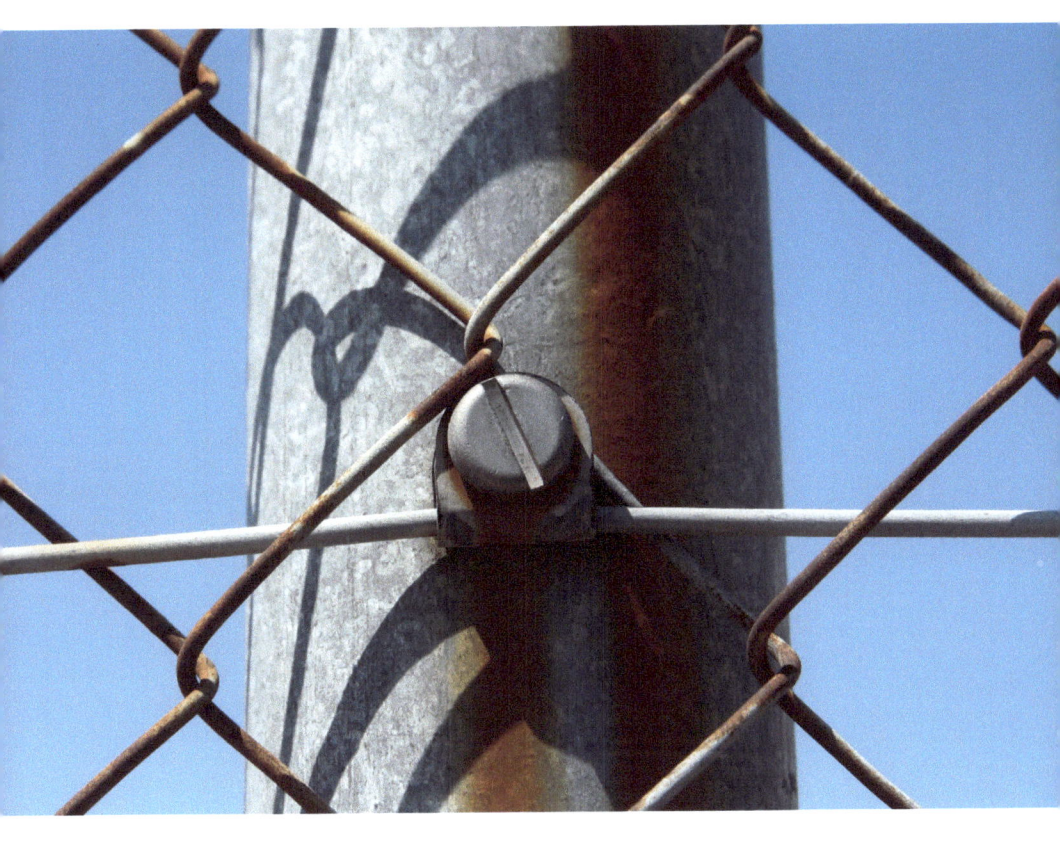

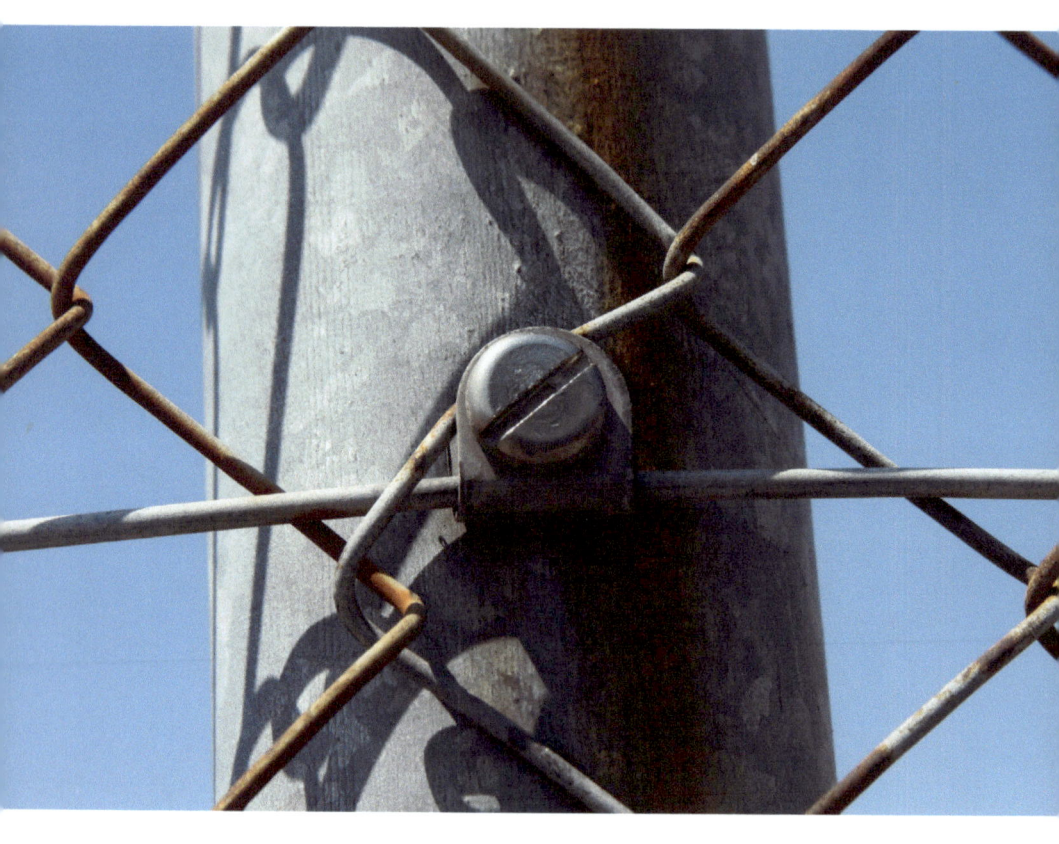

Aesop started again, growing redder, gesturing more broadly, and scaring two rabbits who were hopping along the path.

Normally this would have inspired a delightful rabbit story, but this time Aesop just shouted louder to the fleeing rabbits about a grasshopper and a flea. "And the moral is this," he yelled as the rabbits retreated as fast as they could, "Don't waste resources trying to be somebody you're not."

He slumped onto a log and put his hands in his face and wept.

Were his storytelling days over? What if all his stories began shifting like this? Aesop vowed he would not tell any more stories about things that hopped until he got it sorted out.

After a few minutes he wiped his tears, shook himself, and resumed his walk. He forgot his vow and started over. He was *determined* to get the story right before Athena asked for it again.

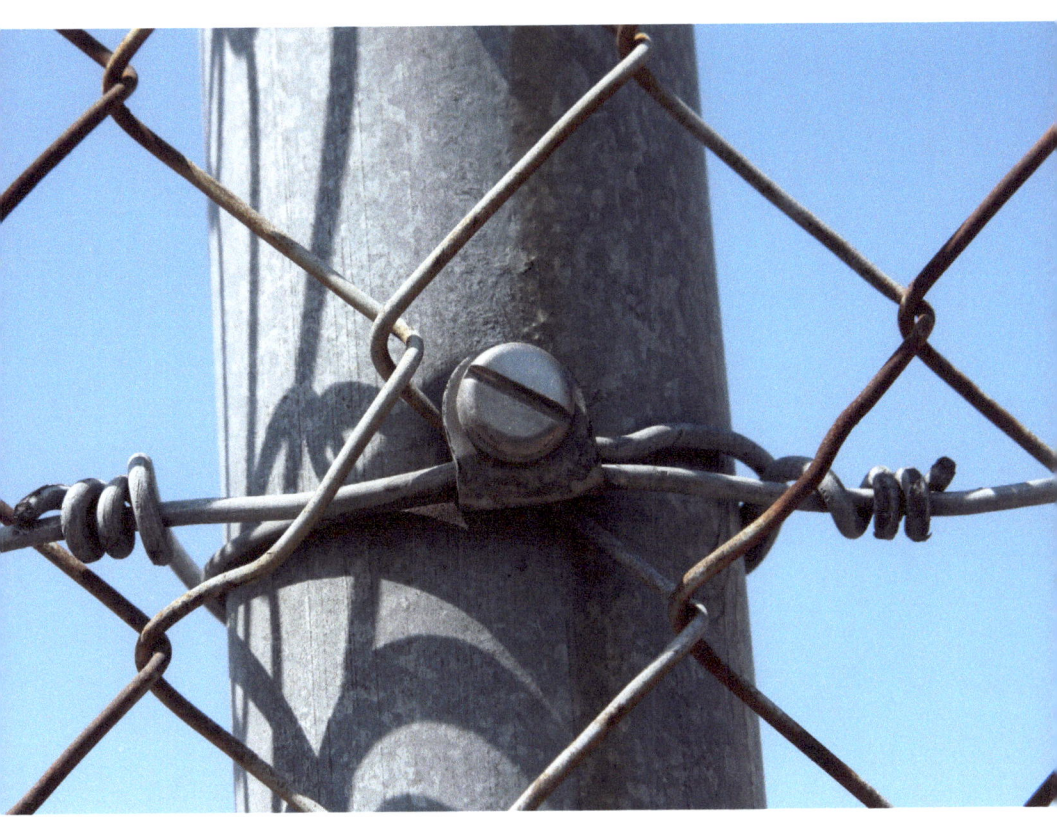

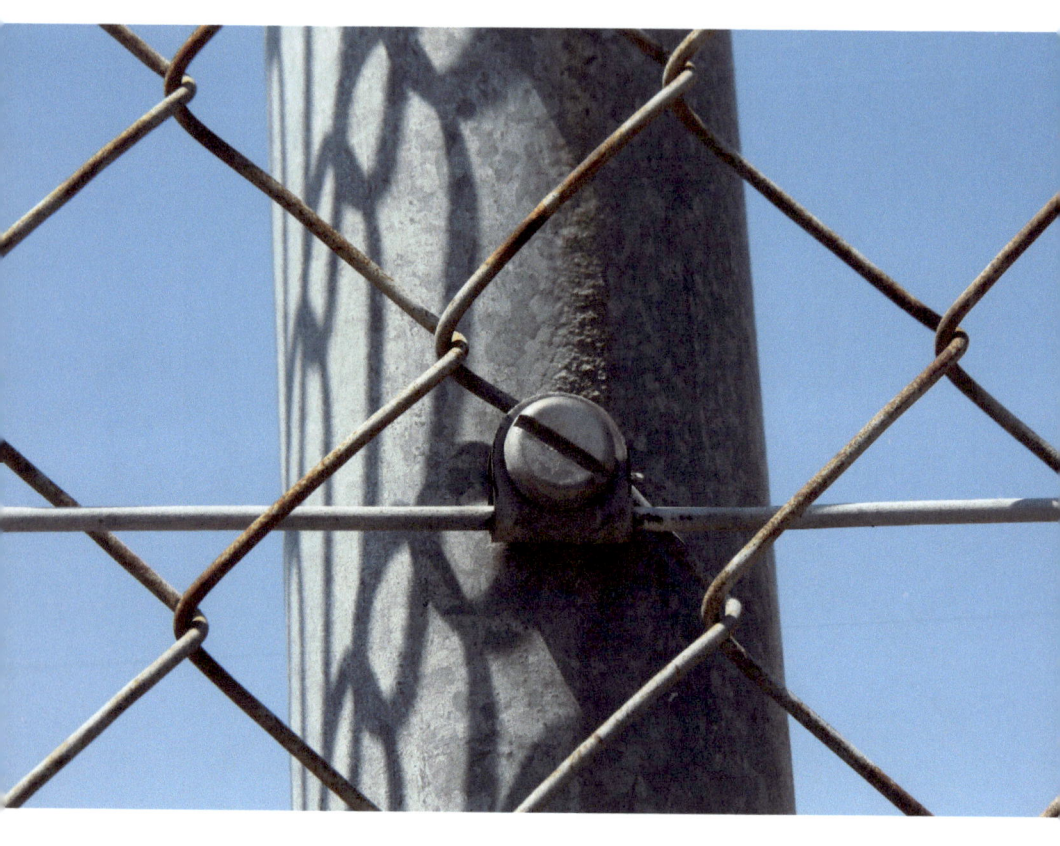

He told the story more than a dozen times, and each time the moral hopped a little. Sometimes it hopped as little as a flea. Sometimes it took a big grasshopper hop. Occasionally it hopped so much Aesop wasn't sure whether it belonged to this story or to some story about two rabbits and a lunatic.

Quite a few morals hopped out of his mouth as the day wore on:

> Your mirror tells who you are, not your neighborhood.

> You'll go farther if you do what comes naturally.

> Fleas with aspirations are still fleas.

> Sometimes you're better off not improving a thing.

> Stop being an idiot.

(This last one wasn't so much a moral to the story as something Aesop yelled at himself for not being able to finish it correctly after so many tries.)

After a while the morals that hopped out of his mouth had less to do with the story itself and more to do with the problem of not being able to pin down the moral:

You can never tell what will happen next.

The first time is sometimes best.

Some truths don't last.

Once is often enough.

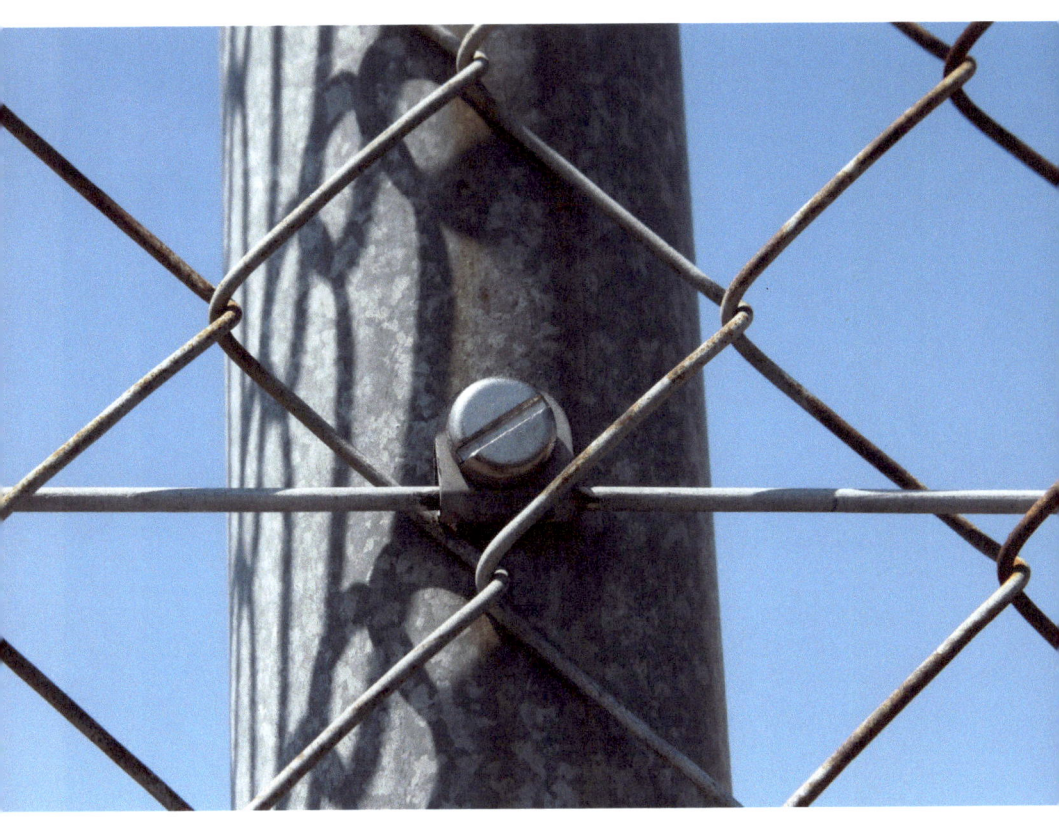

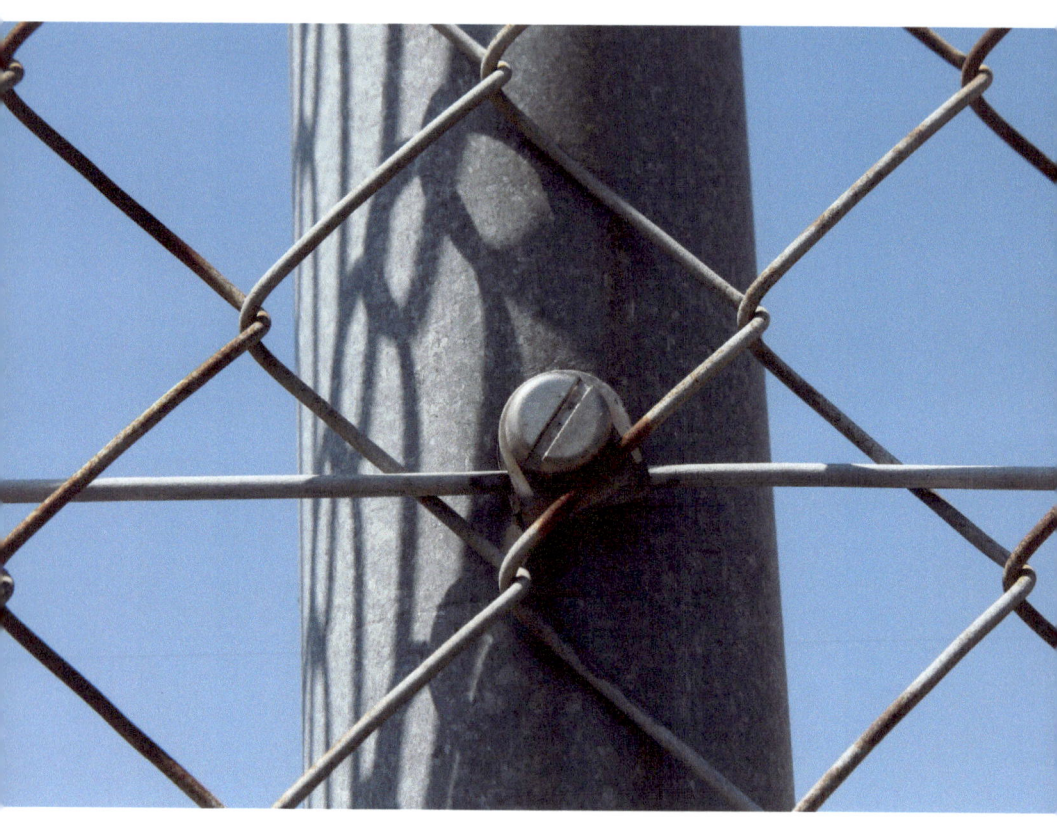

By now any neighbors who encountered Aesop on the country road were surprised at his appearance. He had never been so vexed. He had brought no lunch (he didn't think it would take so long!) and he was quite hungry, but he *loved* Athena and Alex and wanted to please them the next day. So he kept repeating the story, growing more frustrated by the hour.

But it got no better. By the end of the day the hops of the moral were becoming wild, erratic, and large-scale, driven more by his hunger and frustration than anything else

> Eat while you can, for tomorrow you may starve.

> Don't take advice from grasshoppers.

> Morals that hop around reveal more than they should.

> It's no big deal if you go a little crazy now and then.

Aesop practiced until it was dark, but he made no progress and he never once told the story the way Athena and Alex wanted to hear it.

He stumbled home weary and dejected late that night, and told his worried wife that he might have to quit telling fables. She looked at him with concern. "Athena and Alex said you were having trouble with the moral of one of them," she said. Aesop groaned.

"Tell me what it is," she said. "Maybe we can fix it together."

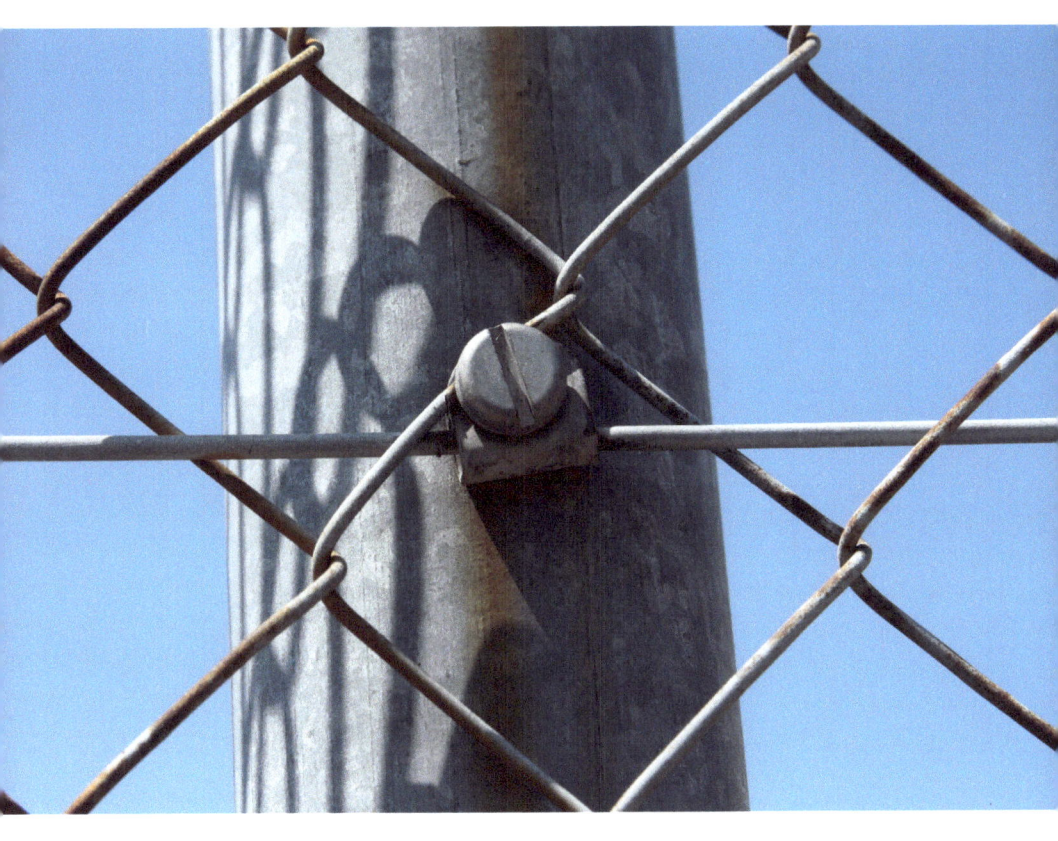

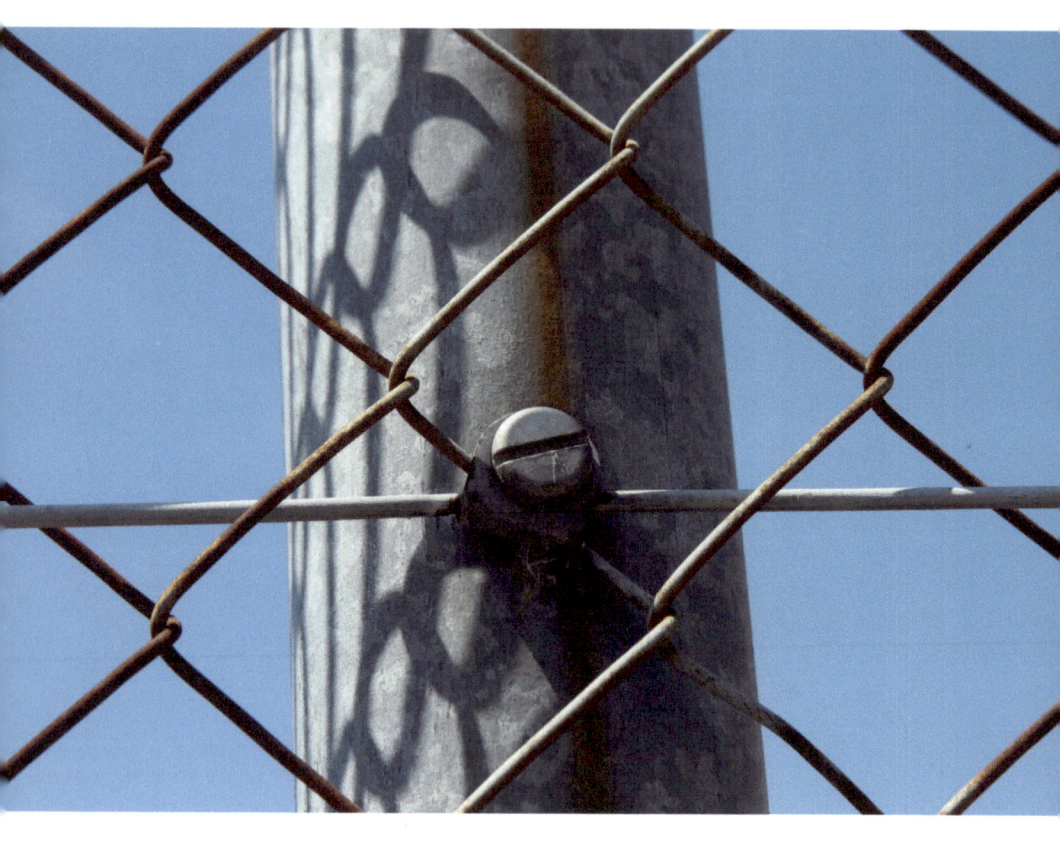

Aesop told her the story of the grasshopper and the flea. "The moral of the story," he concluded, "is that storytellers don't always know what they're talking about."

"Oh," she said laughing. "I've known *that* for a long, long time."

She walked away still laughing, certain that everything would work out soon enough. But Aesop found no comfort in their conversation. He crawled into bed and had a fitful sleep.

The next morning Aesop was slow to get up, so his children (and several children from the neighborhood) all crowded round his bed. "Tell us the story about the flea," Athena said.

"The one with the grasshopper," said Alex. "And tell it right this time."

Aesop moaned. "I'll tell you any story but that one," he said.

"Grasshopper!" said Alex.

"Flea!" said Athena. "Flea! Flea! Flea!"

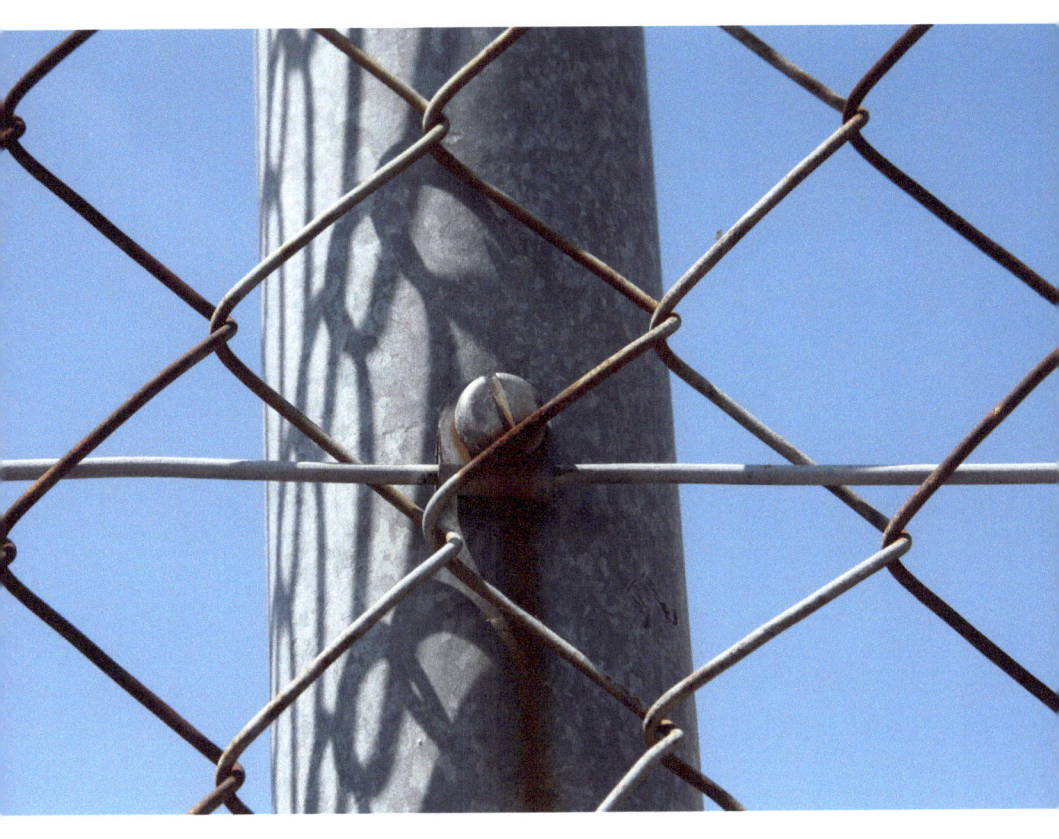

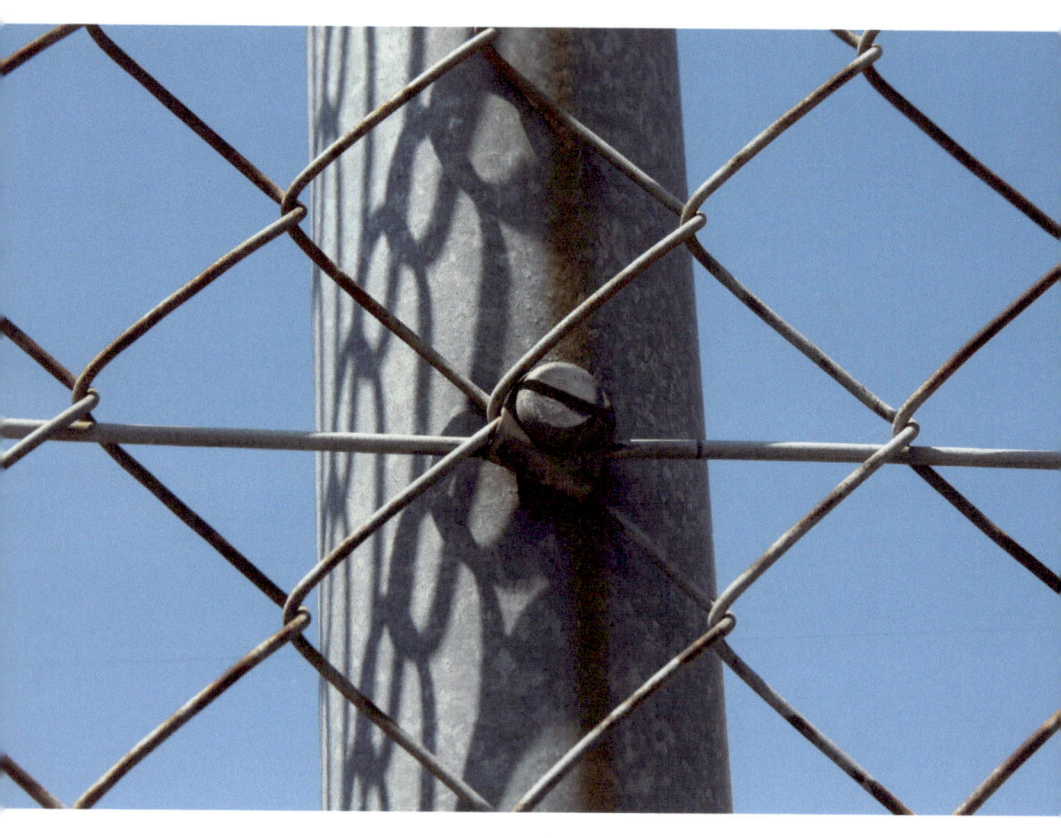

"I *can't!*" Aesop moaned. "I can't say the moral. It keeps changing."

Athena didn't believe her father. "Some things never change," she said. Then she brightened. "You tell the story, and *we'll* say the moral."

Aesop looked at her quizzically. It might work, he thought. "Okay," he said.

He recited the story flawlessly. Just like they wanted to hear it.

"And the moral is," he said, drawing in a big fearful breath, wondering if Athena's moral would hop away also.

"Some things never change!" shouted Athena triumphantly.

"Hurray!" shouted Alex. "Some things never change!"

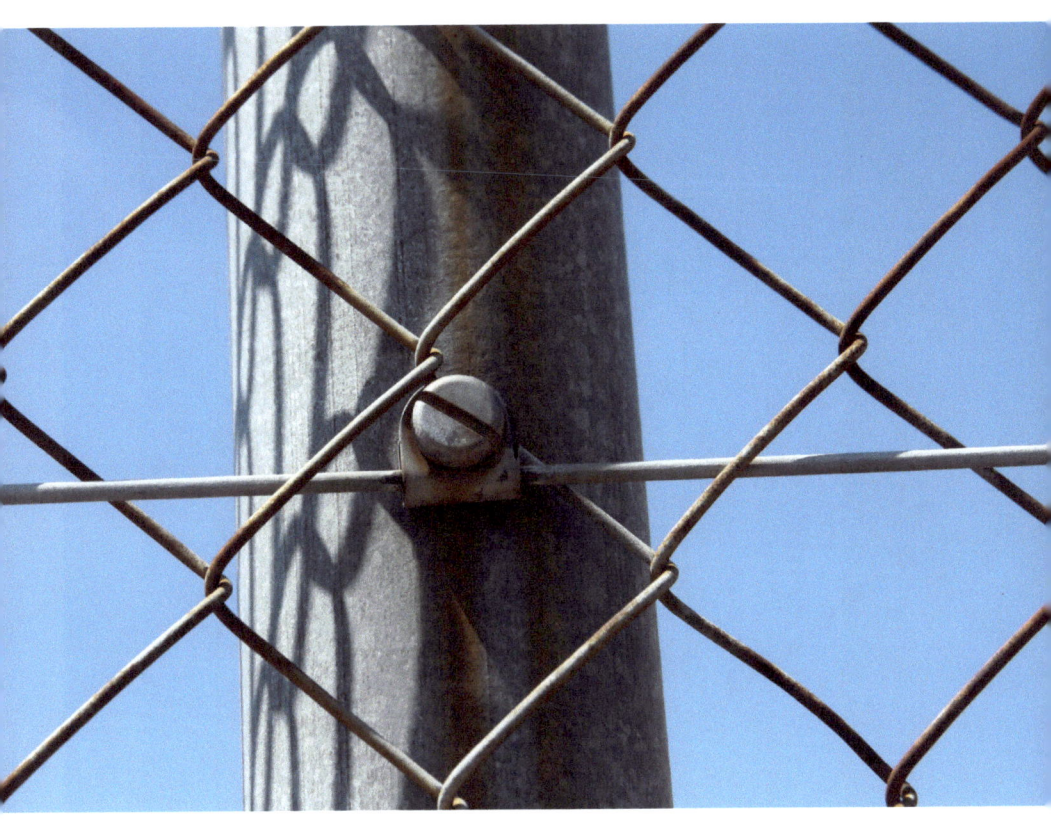

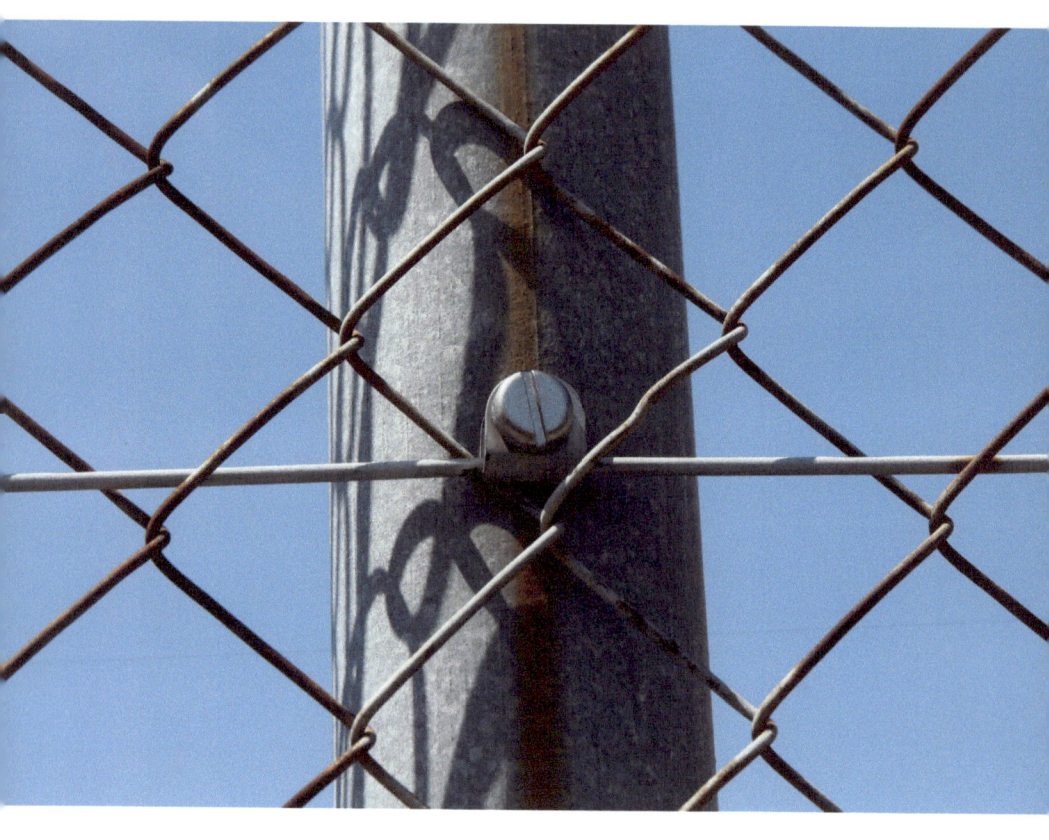

The two youngest ran out to play. Aesop was left with the older kids still standing around his bed, in no hurry to go. His oldest son smiled as he watched Athena and Alex run out to play. Then he turned to his dad.

"I liked it better the old way," he said. "I liked it when you couldn't tell what would happen next."

"*I* didn't," said Aesop. "I didn't like that *at all*."

His son persisted. "What do *you* say the moral is? Today, I mean. What's the moral for this story for today?"

Aesop cleared his throat. He wasn't sure what would hop out of his mouth. He wasn't sure he wanted to know. But he loved his kids and never turned them down when they wanted a story. So he decided to take a chance.

"The moral," he said, "is that sometimes one story has several purposes."

That may have been it. It's hard to remember. It was either that or he said, "The moral is that some stories are hard to pin down."

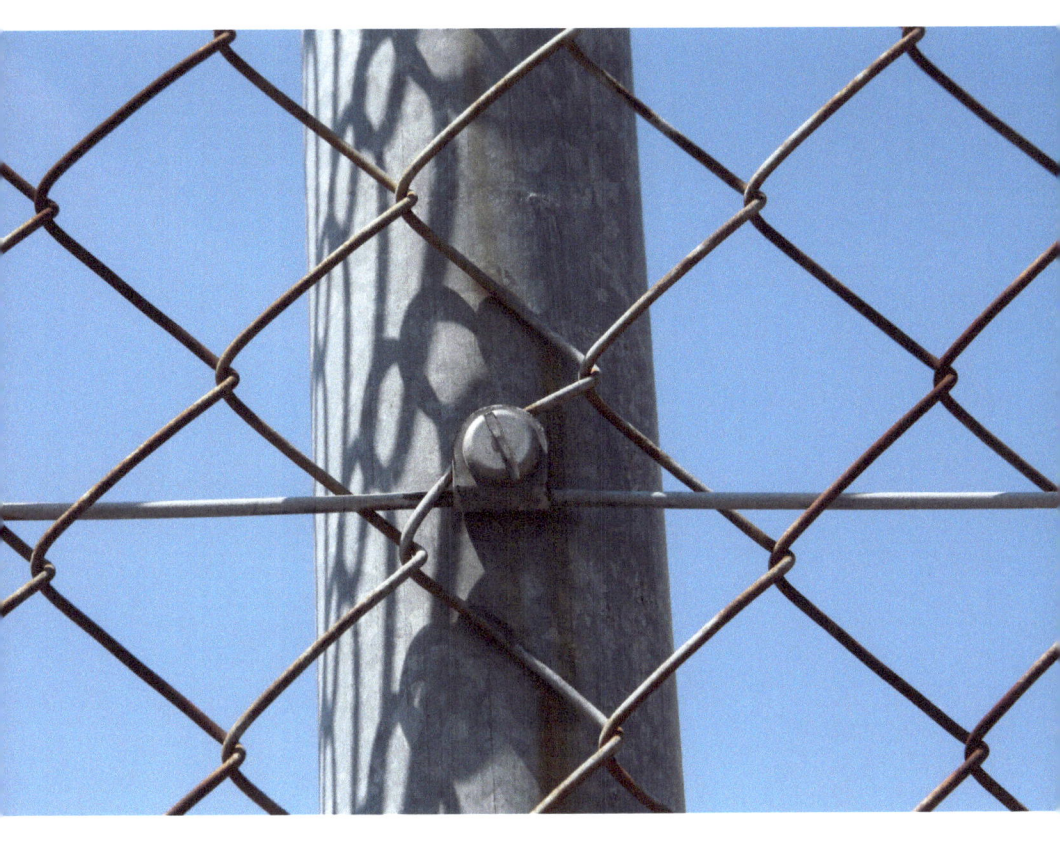

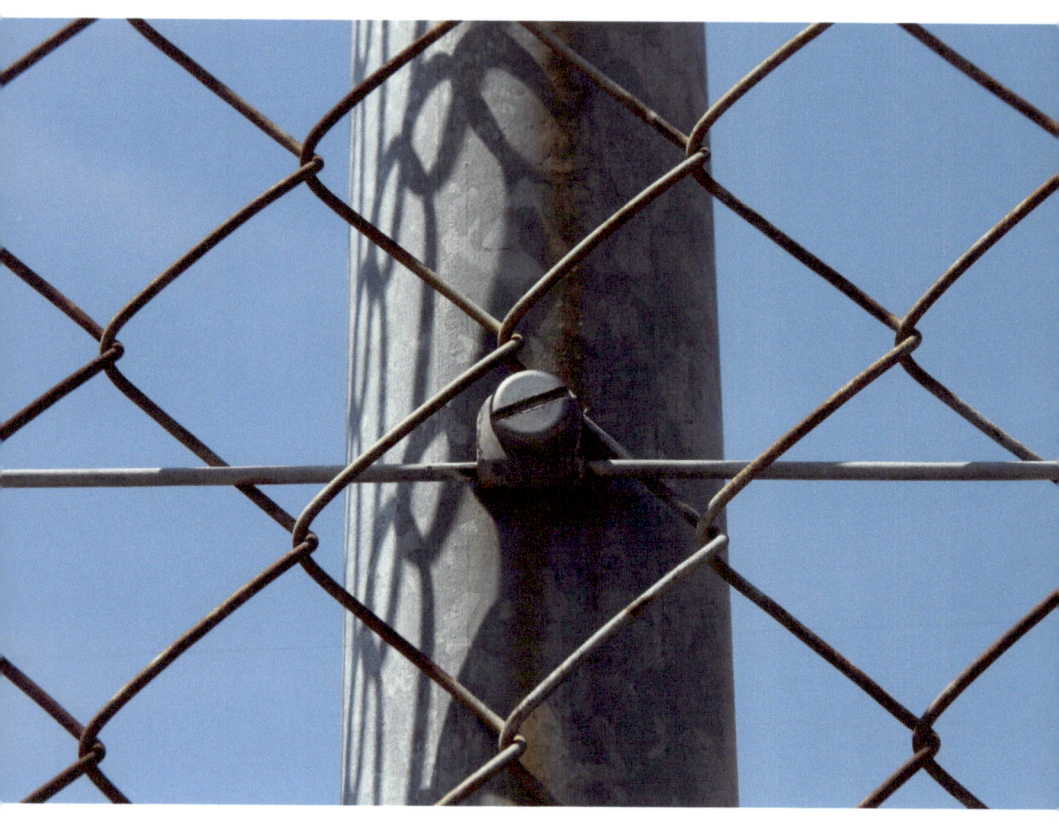

His eldest nodded, and all the rest of the kids ran out to play. Aesop collapsed back on his bed. His eldest looked back before leaving. "Keep it up, dad," he said. "I think you're getting better." Aesop smiled weakly and his son ran out.

Aesop didn't think his story-telling career was over. At least not yet. But he was not going to write down the story of the grasshopper and the flea. Not when it kept hopping around like that.

Instead Aesop started work on a story about two rabbits who met a lunatic out for a walk. By the time Aesop was done, it was the story of the rabbit and the raven. If you haven't heard that one yet, perhaps I'll tell it to you sometime soon.

But just so you know: the last time I checked, the raven had flown away with the moral of that story, so *it* doesn't end all wrapped up, either. Some things never change.

Reflection questions

What do *you* think the moral of Aesop's story about the grasshopper and the flea should be? Today, I mean. What should the moral be today?

What should the moral of the story of your life be, at least for today?

If you decided to improve your life without changing any of the details, what new moral could you give for the story of your life?

After you think of ten morals for the story of your life, choose the one you think might be the most helpful for today. Try it out for a while. You can always change it tomorrow. Probably.

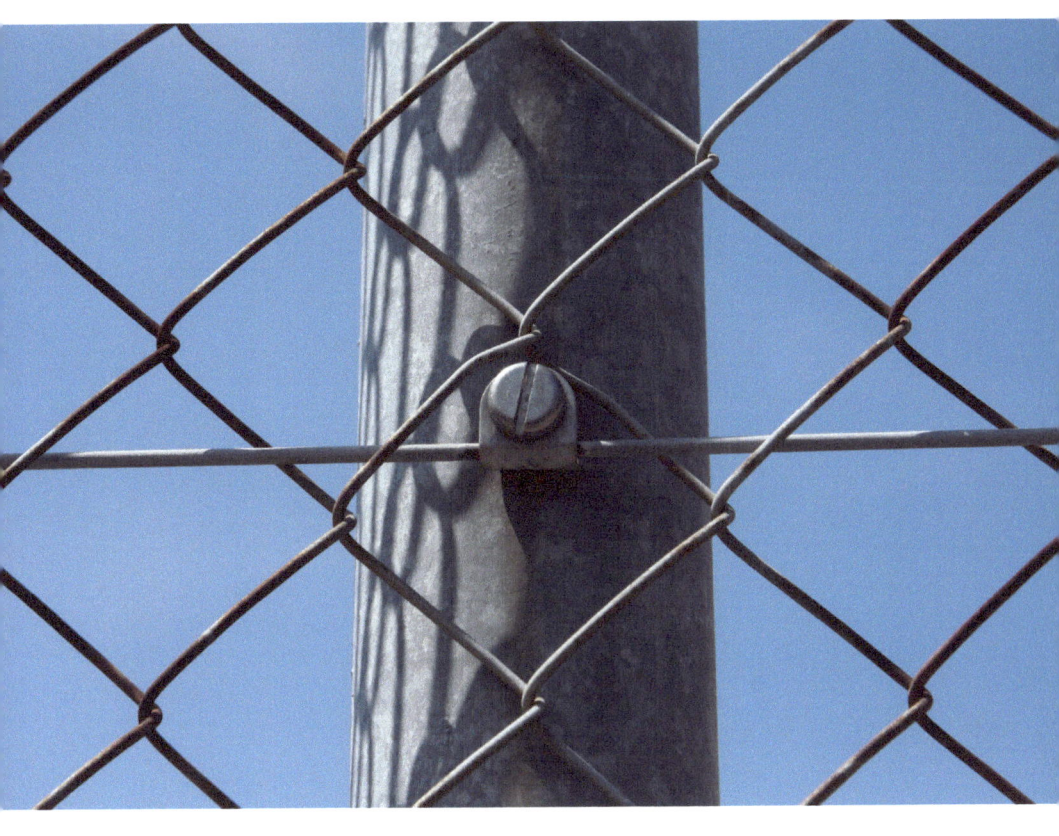

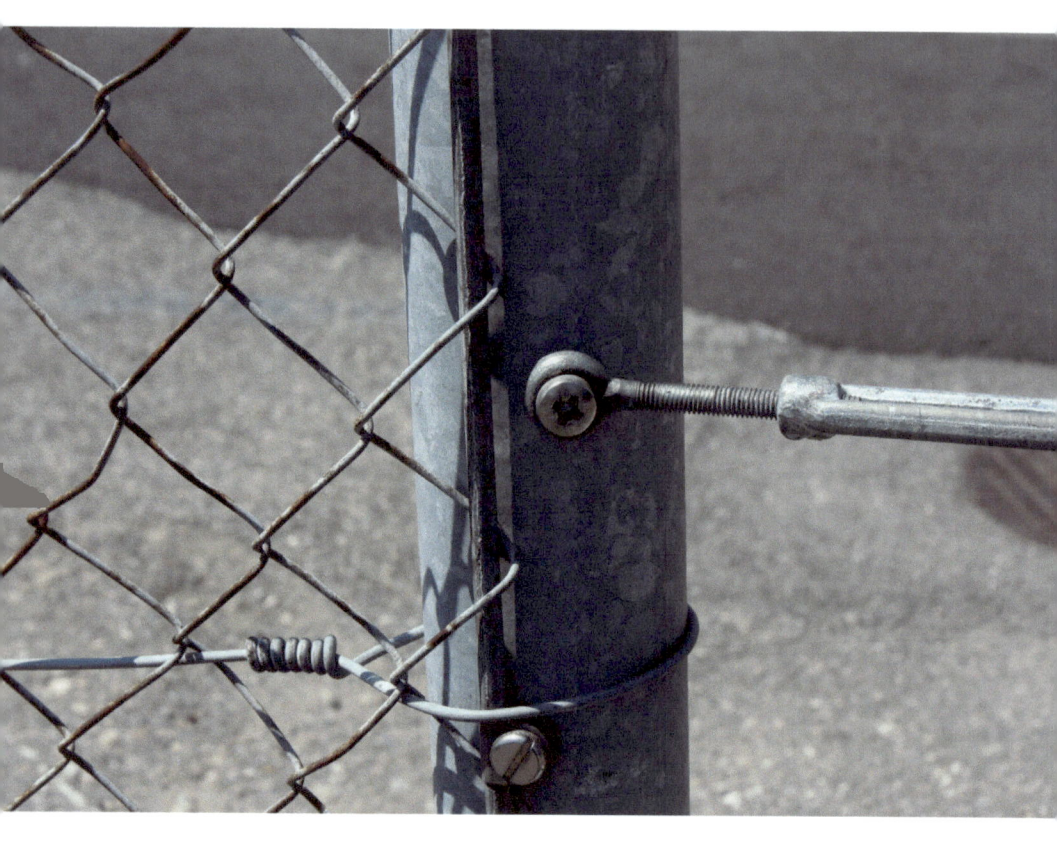

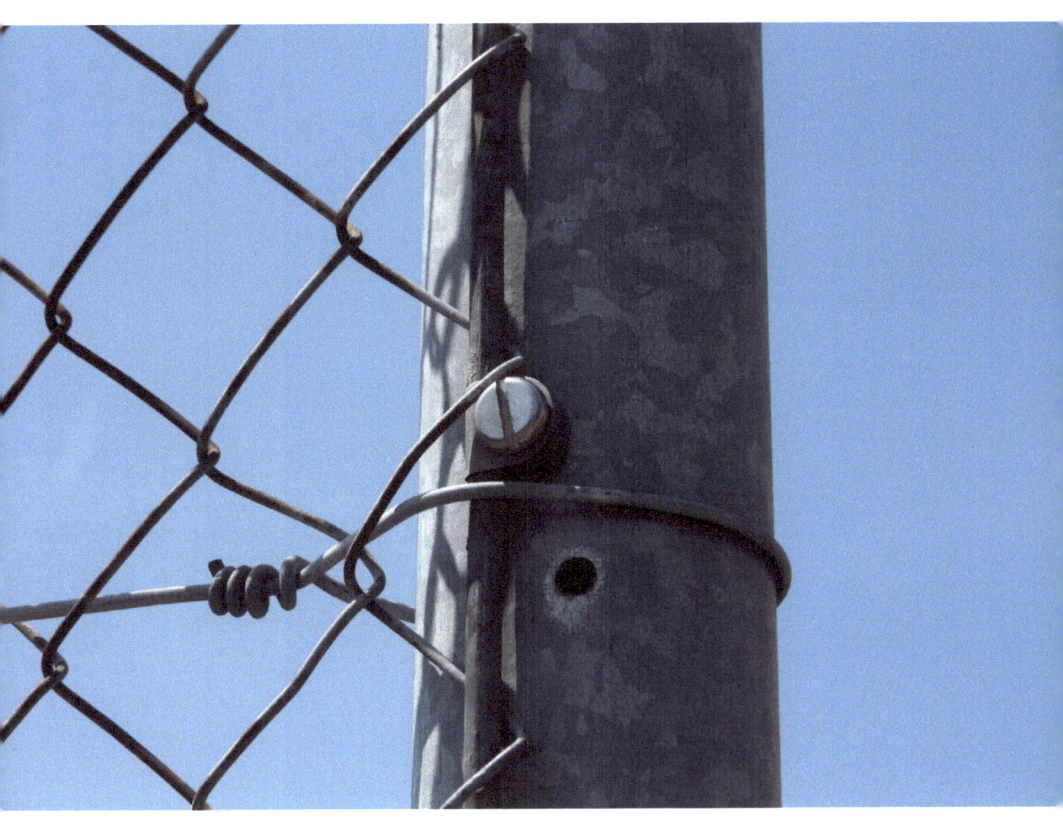

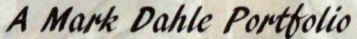

A Mark Dahle Portfolio

Amanda Gets A Pumpkin

(#1 in the series "Amanda Wanted A Miracle")

This Mark Dahle Portfolio includes a colorful painting, twenty-four beautiful industrial photographs from Beijing, Shangahi and Xian, and a story about a girl who wanted a miracle.

"Oh dear," said her grandmother. "You didn't want a pumpkin? Perhaps we'll have to try again."

This Mark Dahle Portfolio includes a colorful painting, twenty-six beautiful photographs from Detroit, and a story about a carpenter who made fine furniture from scraps.

The carpenter came across the twig one day while scouring the countryside for debris. He had already found a sheet of plastic, a broken piece of plywood and several rusty, bent nails. Those he knew he could use. But the twig? He could not imagine a use for it. Nevertheless, it caught his attention as he walked along the edge of a forest. He absentmindedly picked it up.

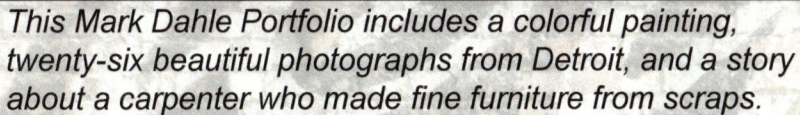

A Mark Dahle Portfolio

The Carpenter And The Twig

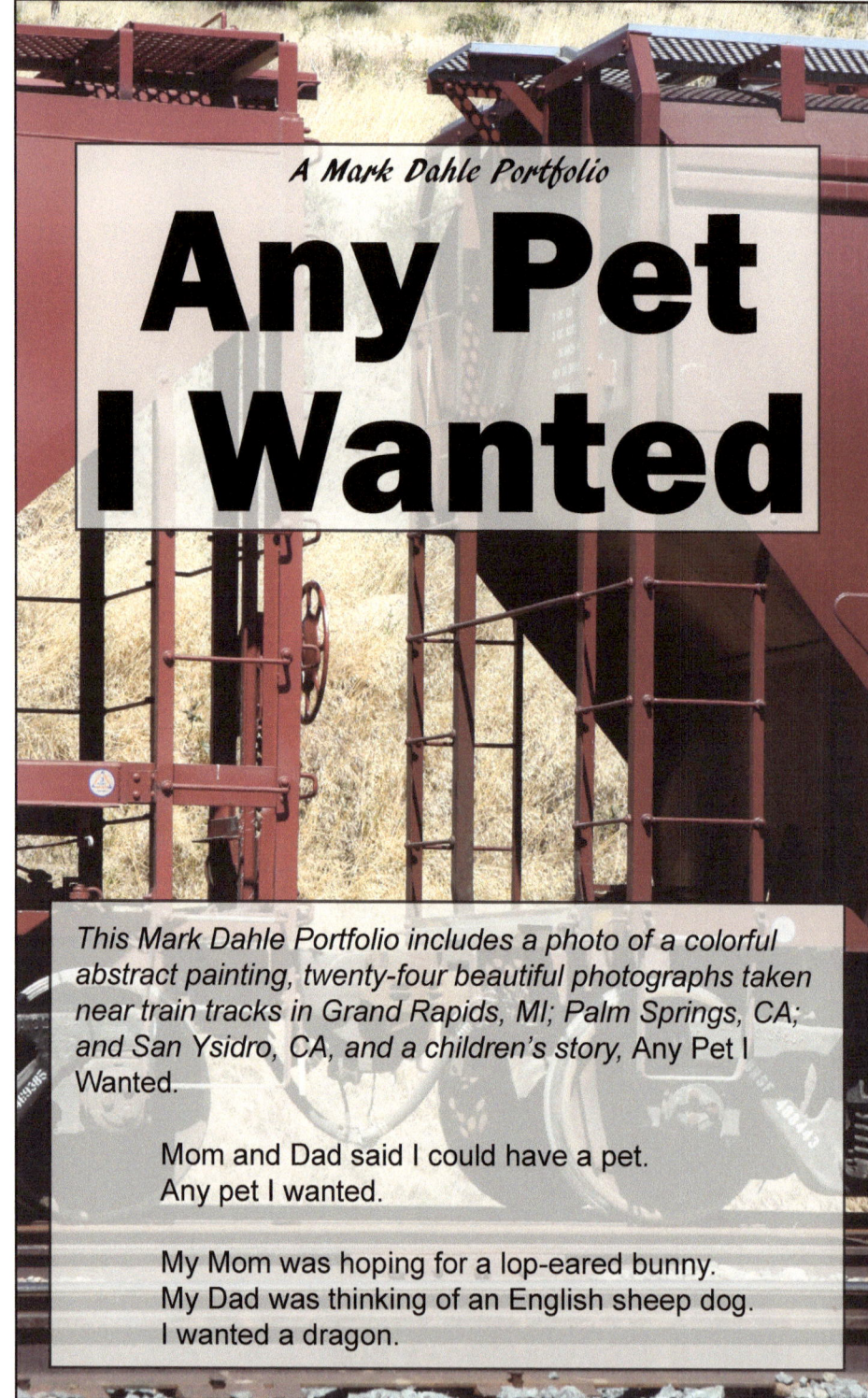

A Mark Dahle Portfolio

Any Pet I Wanted

This Mark Dahle Portfolio includes a photo of a colorful abstract painting, twenty-four beautiful photographs taken near train tracks in Grand Rapids, MI; Palm Springs, CA; and San Ysidro, CA, and a children's story, Any Pet I Wanted.

Mom and Dad said I could have a pet.
Any pet I wanted.

My Mom was hoping for a lop-eared bunny.
My Dad was thinking of an English sheep dog.
I wanted a dragon.

www.ingramcontent.com/pod-product-compliance
Lightning Source LLC
Chambersburg PA
CBHW040857180526
45159CB00001B/445